_____ My Little Boc

THE VOYAGE

NEW SEASONS
PUBLISHING

© 1993 Publications International, Ltd.
ISBN 0-7853-0088-0
Adapted by Etta G. Wilson
Illustrations by Gary Torrisi
Made in the U.S.A.

After Jesus was taken up to heaven, his disciples went on with his mission. They taught all the people they met about Jesus. Now they were called the apostles of Jesus. Many people came to believe in Jesus. They were called "believers" and they would often meet to pray and study together.

The apostles and many believers lived in Jerusalem. But the rulers of the city and a lot of other people did not think Jesus was the Son of God. They hunted for believers and tried to punish them.

One of the people who wanted to catch believers was Saul. He did not want believers to preach about Jesus. Saul went from house to house looking for believers. When he found them, he threw them into jail.

One day, Saul heard there were believers in the city of Damascus teaching about Jesus. Right away, he set out for Damascus with his helpers. He was going to arrest the believers there and bring them back to Jerusalem as prisoners.

On the road to Damascus, a bright light from the sky flashed around Saul! A voice came out of the sky saying, "Saul, Saul, why are you hurting me?"

When Saul asked who was speaking, the voice answered, "I am Jesus! When you hurt my believers, you hurt me too!"

Saul was so afraid that he began to tremble. Jesus spoke to him again. "Go to Damascus and there you will be told what to do." Then the great light disappeared.

Then Saul stood up and opened his eyes. But he could not see a thing! Saul was blind!

His helpers took him by the hand and led him into the city of Damascus. There, Saul thought much about the words of Jesus and the believers whom he had harmed. He did not eat or drink for three days and spent the time praying to God.

While Saul prayed, Jesus sent him a vision, telling him that he would be healed by a believer named Ananias.

After three days, Jesus talked to Ananias in a vision, saying, "Ananias, go to the house of a man named Judas on Straight Street. There you will find a man named Saul. He is waiting for you to make him see again."

Ananias was surprised at Jesus' words. He said, "I have heard terrible things about Saul. I am afraid of him."

Jesus answered, "Go! Do not be afraid of Saul. I have chosen him to be a believer and to teach many people about me."

Ananias left and went to find Saul as he had been told in the vision. When he arrived, he placed his hands on Saul's eyes and said, "Saul, Jesus has sent me. He will heal you today and fill you with his Spirit!"

Suddenly something that looked like fish scales fell from Saul's eyes and he could see again! Then Saul believed that Jesus truly was the Son of God. He was baptized, and then Saul was also a believer!

For several days Saul stayed with believers in Damascus. He began to be called Paul. Right away, he began to preach about Jesus. The people who heard him were amazed. They asked, "Isn't this the same man who searched for believers so he could put them in jail?"

Paul kept preaching that Jesus was the Son of God. But the people who did not believe in Jesus' teachings became angry with Paul. They made plans to kill him when he passed through the gate of the city. They sent guards to watch for Paul there.

When Paul heard about this, he asked other believers for help. After it got dark, the believers lowered Paul over the Damascus city wall in a big basket! And so Paul escaped.

Paul went back to Jerusalem. He wanted to join the believers and apostles there. But the believers in Jerusalem were still afraid of him.

One believer named Barnabas talked with Paul and wanted to help him. Barnabas took Paul with him to meet the apostles. He told them what had happened to Paul on the road to Damascus and how Paul had preached boldly about Jesus in Damascus.

After hearing this, the apostles accepted Paul as a true believer. Paul stayed with them and preached in Jerusalem. But once again, those who did not love Jesus tried to kill Paul.

Finally, the believers sent Paul back to his hometown of Tarsus. They thought he would be safer there.

Later, Barnabas went to Tarsus to see Paul. The two men traveled to many different cities where the people had never heard of Jesus.

One day they arrived at an island called Paphos. There they met a man named Bar-Jesus. He was a magician, and he fooled many people into believing that he knew God's plans. The Governor of Paphos wanted to learn about Jesus. But Bar-Jesus was against this.

Paul was angry. He looked Bar-Jesus in the eye and said, "You are a liar and a cheat. Jesus will make you blind for a while!"

Bar-Jesus fell to the ground, blinded. The Governor of Paphos was amazed. Barnabas and Paul taught the governor about Jesus and he became a believer.

After this, Paul traveled far and wide, teaching about Jesus. In a city called Lystra, he healed a man who had never walked in his life!

Paul preached the same message about God's goodness over a big part of the world. His words and his travels helped many people know Jesus.